# OPERATION 'DESERT SHIELD'

## THE FIRST 90 DAYS

TEXT AND PHOTOS BY

**ERIC MICHELETTI
& YVES DEBAY**

Windrow & Greene

**Eric MICHELETTI**     **Yves DEBAY**

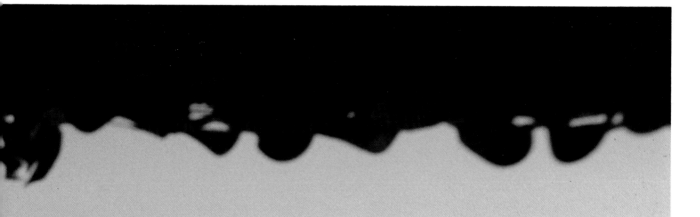

A world of burning sand, under an immense sky of featureless blue. As far as the eye can see in any direction, a perfectly flat horizon which melts into the hem of the sky in a wavering haze. A true hell on earth; but even this dreadful place was not entirely 'forgotten of God'. For the Bedouin have one treasure — 'black gold' . . . a mixed blessing for the nations of the Gulf, and for the great powers overseas.

The Iraqi invasion of Kuwait on 2 August 1990 put Saddam Hussein's tanks within reach of over a quarter of the world's oil reserves. With the unprecedented agreement of almost every member of the United Nations, the USA responded to Saudi Arabia's appeal for support by sending scores of thousands of her best troops half way round the world. They were joined by Egyptian, Syrian, Moroccan, Pakistani and Gulf state forces. Britain quickly sent squadrons of combat jets, later followed by the 120 heavy tanks and nearly 10,000 men of the 7th Armoured Brigade — lineal descendants of Montgomery's 'Desert Rats'. France announced the planned deployment of a 4,000-man brigade. Thirteen navies sent warships to help enforce the UN embargo on Iraq's trade.

We have both accompanied the GIs of America's élite units on peacetime manoeuvers, in Europe and the Near East. Now they were heading into the unknown, on war alert, facing a formidable Arab army in a terrain as hostile as any on earth. We went too.

ERIC MICHELETTI and YVES DEBAY

# TO THE LAND OF THE BLACK GOLD

There was no fanfare to greet them; no smiling girls hung garlands of flowers round the necks of the GIs as they clambered down the steps from the Boeings. But then, there seldom are. Even so, a crusade was beginning; it didn't take much imagination to believe one could hear the slow chords of *The Star-Spangled Banner* in the distance. You only had to look at their faces, and the way they carried themselves: America, in all her might, was there. And in all her confidence: as the boys of the 101st Airborne and the 24th Infantry Division tramped across the tarmac of Saudi Arabia's Dhahran airport, they shouted that 'Saddam had better watch out, or they'd go all the way to Baghdad and dig him out of his hole!' Around them the jets of the huge Galaxy transports roared, as mountainous loads of supplies grew beside the runways. Slightly dumbfounded and vaguely uneasy, the Arab world was getting its first look at the soldiers of the New World who had come, so sure of themselves, to help defend the black gold of the Gulf.

Troopers of the 101st Airborne Division (Air Assault) arrive at Dhahran airbase, Saudi Arabia. In less than two hours (after being ordered to drink a litre-and-a-half of mineral water each, within fifteen minutes), they will be heading out into the desert. *(Photo: E.Micheletti)*

Never, since the D-Day landings in Normandy on 6 June 1944, has such a large army been transported so far, to disembark so quickly in a foreign land. Even at the height of the Vietnam War the maritime supply lines and the 'air bridge' were less massive, and less rapid, than in this extraordinary logistic operation.

During the first week of the American intervention a huge Galaxy or Starlifter transport aircraft was landing at one of the airbases of eastern Saudi Arabia on average every fifteen minutes.

In less than six weeks something like 120,000 men had been airlifted in, while another 30,000 were already in position on shipboard in the Persian Gulf.

The fast transport ships were meanwhile unloading over the quays of Saudi Arabia's eastern ports equipment and supplies equivalent to five full divisions. In less than twenty-four hours each ship was unloaded, its cargo of vehicles readied for use and rolling out towards the desert bases — protected from any attack by more than 500 combat jets and as many helicopters.

# THE 'INSTANT ARMY'

A parade of Chinook transport helicopters on the dockside at the port of Damman. In less than a day all these choppers were on their way out into the desert. *(Photo: E. Micheletti)*

**(Opposite top)** Vehicles of the 197th Infantry Brigade (Mechanised) (Separate), from XVIII Airborne Corps, are unloaded from the fast transport ship USS *Denebola*.

**(Right)** Carried by civilian jumbo-jets, the 14,000 troopers of the 101st landed at the same time as their choppers. This completely airmobile division can even lift its own artillery behind enemy lines, supported by its own tactical air units.
*(Photos: Y. Debay)*

A good example was the fast supply ship USS *Denebola*. In just six hours she disembarked at Damman 'more than half the vehicles of the 197th Infantry Brigade. This equipment had left Fort Benning sixteen days before. The troops of the unit arrived a week before their equipment, to acclimatise themselves to the fierce conditions and to start preparing their combat positions.

The whole enormous transport infrastructure was orchestrated on a global scale, forming a kind of gigantic puzzle into which each piece was fitted at the exact time and place selected for it.

**(Below)** Infantry of the 197th Brigade; they had been issued with desert equipment during their journey — right down to a manual explaining how to avoid misunderstandings with the local population.

# EQUAL OPPORTUNITIES ?

Is American public opinion ready to accept the spectacle of young women — perhaps young mothers — being killed in battle wearing US uniform? A coldly military calculation of the probable casualties if the Gulf Crisis turned into a shooting war suggests a mortality rate among US servicewomen in the region of perhaps 5 per cent. Since there are now an estimated 15,000 women present, that percentage has sobering implications.

Even though current US law forbids 'routine engagement in direct combat' by female personnel, their presence in support units close behind the forward edge of battle — and the inevitable blurring between 'front' and 'rear' in modern warfare — puts their lives in jeopardy.

The women's proper role is hotly debated. Feminists, arguing for complete equality of military roles, risks and opportunities, cite the successful combat forced by circumstances upon Capt. Linda Bray's 989th Military Police Co. in Panama in December 1989. They also quote the case of Sgt. Rhonda Maskus, an intelligence analyst with

(Below) Though the majority are employed in non-combatant units, the US servicewomen are trained to handle all standard weapons — like this M60A2 machine gun, mounted on a Humvee light vehicle.

(Right) The USAF has numerous female radar operators, mechanics, missile maintenance crews, and other specialists at Dhahran airbase. (Far right) A female US Army 'Spec 4' assures the security of a Patriot missile launcher system. (Photos: Y. Debay)

82nd Airborne who had specialised on Panama for years, but who was barred from that operation in favor of less qualified men. There is strong support for the feminist position from public opinion polls — but then, the body-bags have not yet started coming home. Another school of thought argues that the presence of 225,000 women in the services causes complications which weaken the forces' readiness; and that in combat male personnel would be distracted, to their peril, by instinctive protective impulses.

While the debate continues, the barriers continue to come down. Currently the medical branch has 39% female officers and 13% non-commissioned and enlisted personnel; in the administrative branches the figures are 14% and 35% respectively. Women in Saudi Arabia serve not just as nurses and clerks, but as truck drivers, communications specialists, traffic patrol crews, and in many other jobs which make them potential targets. Their response is characteristic: 'I signed up for the Army, not the Girl Scouts . . .'

# JUST ANOTHER DAY . . .

It is 8.30 in the morning and the heat is already crushing. Since they arrived in this desert, which is as flat as a pool table, they have had to get accustomed to temperatures of 80°F even at night, and 120° during the day.

Around their positions those troopers who are not on duty sleep, or play cards. The flies, apparently undeterred by the ceaseless desert wind, are already swarming and clinging everywhere you look. After a brisk jog at 5.30 a.m. — an excellent way of clearing the head and toning up the digestion in these latitudes, so they tell you — the GIs have had breakfast: generous portions of something that approximates to real food for the rear echelons, and something out of a plastic pouch for the front line positions. Now, for the hundredth time, they patiently strip and clean their weapons, and test the electronic equipment — which suffers worst of all in these conditions. The sand is as fine as talcum, and finds its way into every crevice. On the program for this morning: an acclimatisation march in full equipment ('just a little walk in the sun . . . ') followed by a live firing exercise.

During their first days in-country each man drank nearly a litre of water an hour. Now they are hardened: seven or eight litres last them twenty-four hours. To us, their morale seemed unshakable; Uncle Sam has sent his best soldiers into this wilderness.

(Far left) In the US forces, nothing is left to mere improvisation: USAF personnel file through a field service chow shack to collect their breakfast. *(Photo: Y. Debay)*

(Left) In this climate it is impossible to swallow pork and beans without a good swill of coffee. It doesn't taste much like home-brewed, but at least it's plentiful. *(Photo: E.Micheletti)*

(Below left) Despite their fatigue, paratroopers of the 82nd Airborne just back from a night patrol carefully clean their M16A2 rifles. The powdery sand is the GIs' inescapable enemy. *(Photo: Y. Debay)*

(Right) Only the USAF personnel on their airbases can enjoy the luxury of a table and benches to eat at. *(Photo: E. Micheletti)*

(Below) The essential link with home: a letter to Mom, wife or girlfriend, scribbled from the patio of 'Heartbreak Hotel — Plenty of Vacancies . . . ' *(Photo: Y. Debay)*

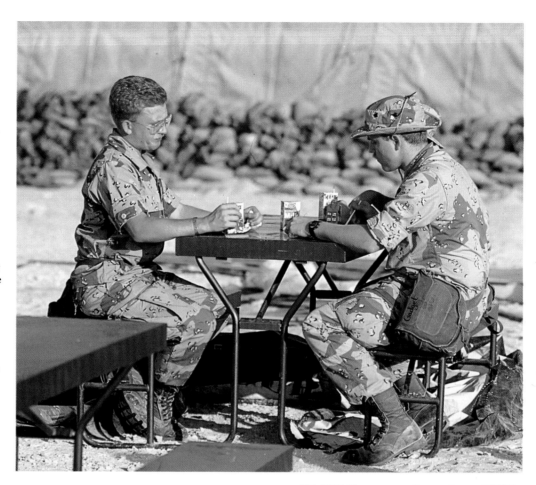

# . . . AT 120°F

## 'THE COMPANY STORE'

At the end of September 1990 the presence of some 120,000 US troops in the Saudi desert meant a daily demand for many hundreds of thousands of gallons of water, provided by Saudi Arabia's 28 desalinisation plants.

The GIs had also consumed a total of around 4,000 tons of meat, plus 3,000 tons of poultry and milk. Some 306,000 bottles of sun cream had been issued, at a cost of $414,000; and 247,000 pairs of special desert sunglasses had been provided ($588,000). The care of the GIs' extremities had been assured by the provision of 600,000 sticks of lip salve, and 400,000 issues of anti-perspirant lotion for the feet ($77,000).

Hundreds of American firms had been mobilised to meet the enormous demands of the Defense Personnel Support Center, the Pentagon's specialist purchasing agency, for everything from chickens to desert-camouflaged uniforms (75,000 ordered), chemical warfare protection suits (450,000 to be delivered by the end of the year), and — of course — individual combat rations (3.4 million packs). Out in the desert, this was one thing the boys did not have to worry about. 'Uncle' could be trusted to provide — and on time.

AIRBORNE

1

3

2

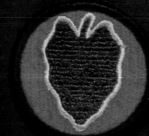

4

5

6

7

8

9

HELL ON WHEELS

2

BRAVE RIFLES

3

# THE INSIGNIA

We illustrate opposite the shoulder patches of most of the major formations of the US Army with elements present in the Gulf in October 1990. They are illustrated in their full-color parade or walking-out versions; on combat clothing they are worn in 'subdued' black and olive versions.

(1)   101st Airborne Division (Air Assault)
(2)   82nd Airborne Division
(3)   24th Infantry Division (Mechanised)
(4)   197th Infantry Brigade (Mechanised) (Separate)
(5)   3rd Armored Cavalry Regiment
(6)   11th Air Defense Artillery Brigade
(7)   1st Logistic Command
(8)   2nd Armored Division
(9)   1st Cavalry Division

(Right) Photographed just after disembarking from a civilian airliner after more than 30 hours en route, an airman of the USAF displays the patch of the 18th Aviation Brigade. *(Photo: Y. Debay)*

(Below left) This paratrooper of the 82nd wears the divisional 'A-A' patch and 'Airborne' title, and above them a personal qualification title — 'Ranger'. *(Photo: Y. Debay)*

(Below right) Waiting for the wheels: a trooper of the 197th Inf. Bde. (Mech.) (Sep.) on the quayside at Damman. *(Photo: E. Micheletti)*

## THE 'SAND-TAGGERS'

'Tags' of every kind have broken out like a rash all over the American installations in Saudi Arabia. The smallest panel, the most out-of-the-way corner of a wall immediately blossoms with wry graffiti. On the 'Christmas tree' signposts humor, fantasy and homesickness blend in a picturesque cocktail. *(Photo: E. Micheletti)*

(Below) LCDR Roach, official artist to the American expeditionary force, designing the future insignia of Operation 'Desert Shield'. *(Photo: Y.Debay)*

Scout paratroopers of the 82nd Airborne stretching their legs outside the confines of their LAV armored vehicle. Note the body armor, particularly uncomfortable under the desert sun. *(Photo: E.Micheletti)*

# UP TO THE LINE

(Above) Men of an 82nd Airborne mortar squad de-truck from their GMC to take part in a desert march and combat exercise several miles from their lines. Physical fitness and stamina, always fundamental to these troops, are especially vital in these extreme climatic conditions. *(Photo: E.Micheletti)*

(Left) An officer of the 24th Infantry Division. The desert camouflage uniform in tan and sand is speckled with black and white random spots to mimic the shadows and highlights of the scattered stones so typical of desert terrain. *(Photo: Y.Debay)*

(Right) For those with an eye for 20th century military history, this silhouette recalls the French soldier in Algeria 30 years ago. Like soldiers everywhere, this pensive GI has tried to bring a touch of individuality to his bush hat; its brim is not quite large enough for a true 'gunslinger' effect . . . *(Photo: E.Micheletti)*

(Below) Squinting into the immense desert distances, a paratrooper of the 82nd watches a platoon of the division's Sheridan recce tanks from the 3/73rd Armor deploy over a terrain which has not changed since the time of Tamerlane's hordes. *(Photo: Y.Debay)*

(Above) Live firing exercise with the infantry's basic weapons: M16A2 rifle, M249 SAW squad light machine gun, and 84mm AT-4 rocket launcher.

(Left) M102 howitzer, caliber 105mm, in its camouflaged firing position. This divisional artillery piece is light enough to be transported by air, slung beneath a chopper.

(Right) These troopers of the 82nd carry the M249 Squad Automatic Weapon in 5.56mm, as issued to one man in every four-man fire team (foreground); the M60A2 machine gun, limited in the infantry to the company's weapons platoon — here it has just been dismounted from a Humvee vehicle; and the corporal team leader's M203, an M16 rifle with integral 40mm grenade launcher, useful out to 350 meters.
(Photos: Y.Debay)

# M102 LIGHT HOWITZER

The 105mm M102 appeared in 1964, and later saw service in the Vietnam War. 1,200 examples have been produced by the Rock Island Arsenal. It is currently being replaced in Active Component units by the M119, but is still in service with the 82nd and 101st Divisions and other light units. In the airborne formations each Artillery Battalion has three batteries each of six guns.

**Crew**: Eight **Weight**: 3,310 lbs.
**Length**: 17 ft. **Rate of Fire**: 10 rpm
**Range**: 11,500 meters with conventional HE ammunition; 15,500 m with rocket-assisted ammunition

General Norman Schwarzkopf, commanding the Kuwait Task Force, is a giant of a man — 6 ft. 3 ins. and 240 lbs. — who enjoys the nickname of 'the Bear'; but there is nothing slow about his understanding. He quickly grasped that the only way his boys could avoid getting bogged down — literally and figuratively — was to manoeuver constantly over the face of the desolate moonscape which would be their zone of operations if 'Desert Shield' led to actual combat. The sand can grind down men's morale as badly as it abrades their equipment: it must be confronted, and mastered.

After a week for acclimatisation, during which marches and weapons exercises are carried out at a pace adapted to the conditions, things get serious again. This is particularly true of the paratroopers, who were the first to arrive in Arabia. Practice approach marches and combat exercises alternate in a relentless rhythm with live firing, helicopter lifts, and combined assaults with armored vehicles. There is no way of knowing exactly what combat mission may be thrown at the 82nd if Iraq takes the ultimate gamble; but they will be familiar with the terrain and the possible 'plays', and professionalism will do the rest.

(Right) Live firing practice for a trooper armed with the M249 SAW; each squad of 12 men plus a sergeant squad leader is divided into three four-man teams, one man with a SAW, one with an M203, and two with basic M16 rifles. All can carry one or two AT-4 launchers in addition. The SAW, a licence-built version of a Belgian design, has a rate of fire of 1,000 rpm.

*(Photos: Y. Debay)*

The 82nd Airborne train relentlessly in the combat techniques particular to this eery terrain. If any World War 2 GI had been shown this picture, he would have thought it was a still from a science fiction movie; the appearance of the American footslogger has changed out of all recognition even in the past 20 years.

(Right) An F-15C pilot of the 1st Tactical Fighter Wing returns from a mission, his face marked by the pressure of his oxygen mask. *(Photo: E.Micheletti)*

(Below) On the runway, an Eagle pilot awaits the order to take off. In a few moments he will begin his long vigil under the control of Dhahran radar. *(Photo: E.Micheletti)*

(Opposite) An Eagle of the 1st TFW soars into the Arabian skies ahead of the howl of its two turbofans. For four hours this pilot and his wingman will patrol watchfully along the Saudi-Iraqi border. *(Photo: Y.Debay)*

(Opposite below) The insignia of the 1st TFW; these new 'desert eagles' are normally based at Langley AFB, Virginia. *(Photo: E.Micheletti)*

# THE DESERT EAGLES

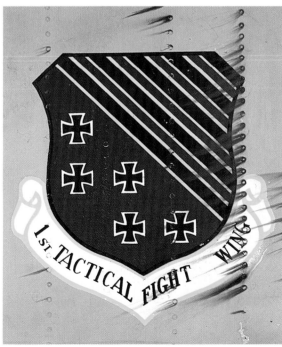

Ten minutes past seven in the morning: the sun is already radiating off the concrete surfaces of Dhahran's enormous airbase facilities with uncomfortable strength. Between the hardened walls of a sand-colored aircraft dispersal pen the two Pratt & Whitney jets of an F-15C fighter are howling. The last nods and signals of confirmation pass between the pilot and his ground crew. In ten minutes he will be airborne with his wingman, relieving two other pilots of the 1st Tactical Fighter Wing who have already been patrolling the skies of Arabia for four hours.

Each F-15C Eagle interceptor is armed with eight air-to-air missiles: four short-range AIM-9L Sidewinders, an infra-red 'fire and forget' plane killer which can lock onto a target at any angle of approach; and four of the older AIM-7F Sparrows, which can be fired at up to 30 miles' range, but which have the disadvantage that the pilot has to continue to 'bathe' the target with his radar until the missile itself locks on several seconds after firing. Together, and backed by a 20mm 'Gatling gun', they represent a mix of weaponry to give pause to any Iraqi MiG-29 or Su-24 pilot.

The flower of America's fighter and bomber units have flown to the Gulf from all over the USA and Europe: F-16 Falcons of the 401st TFW from Torrejon, Spain; F-111s of the 48th TFW from Lakenheath, England; F-15E strike aircraft of the 336th TFS, 4th TFW from Seymour Johnson, North Carolina . . . And embarked off-shore are their counterparts of the carrier groups: F-14 Tomcats, F-18 Hornets, A-6 Intruders — and the V/STOL AV-8 Harrier 'jump-jets' of the US

Marines. With the support of B-52s from Diego Garcia, and F-117 Stealth fighters from Turkish bases, plus electronic warfare aircraft like the EA-6 Prowler and F-4G Wild Weasel, the US task force has a balanced air fleet of more than 800 aircraft.

**(Left) Apart from the rotating double patrols, four aircraft are kept at constant readiness on the ground to react to the first sign of enemy air activity.** *(Photo: E.Micheletti)*

## McDONNELL DOUGLAS F-15C EAGLE

## AIR SUPERIORITY

## FIGHTER

**Crew:** One
**Maximum speed:** 1,680 mph
**Powerplant:** Two Pratt & Whitney F100-PW-220 turbofans
**Empty weight:** 12.8 tons
**Loaded weight:** 19.7 tons
**Length:** 63.6ft. **Height:** 18.3 ft.
**Wing span:** 42.6 ft.
**Armament:** One M61A1 20mm rotary cannon, four AIM-7F Sparrow and four AIM-9L Sidewinder air-to-air missiles

Crouched in a hardened concrete dispersal pen holding four fighters, an F-15C gets ready to roll. *(Photo: E.Micheletti)*

The most trying phase of duty, for pilot and aircraft alike: 'stand-by' on the baking concrete of Dhahran. *(Photo: Y.Debay)*

(Above) The extreme climatic conditions of the Gulf can play hell with sophisticated electronic systems. The Eagles at Dhahran are given frequent inspections in the base hangars to ensure constant readiness.

(Right) 1st TFW armorers check the deadly AIM-9L Sidewinders which are the Eagle's primary air-to-air weapons. On the lower rails of the trolley are Martin Marietta laser guidance pods, as fitted to the F-15E.

*(Photos: Y.Debay)*

BAe Hawk Mk.60 of the RSAF. These versatile machines double as both advanced trainers and useful ground attack assets in Saudi service. *(Photo: Y.Debay)*

# THE ROYAL SAUDI AIR FORCE

The Royal Saudi Air Force has a total of 180 combat aircraft. Most are US-built, although in recent years the RSAF has also fielded two (soon, three) squadrons each of 20 British Tornado strike aircraft. The strike force is completed by three squadrons each of 20 F-15E Eagles.

There are three interceptor squadrons with a total of 42 F-15C Eagles armed with AIM-9L air-to-air and AGM-65 air-to-ground missiles. In a part of the world whose terrain is perfect for radar surveillance, the Saudis have recently bought five Boeing E-3A AWACS machines.

The kingdom also has a large fleet of modern helicopters, including recently delivered Black Hawks identical to those flown by the US Army. Training types include the British Aerospace Hawk Mk.

60, which has a useful ground-attack capability. A significant transport fleet includes 33 C-130 Hercules, nine L-100s and 35 C-212s.

A high state of readiness is maintained by a large number of European and American contract technicians; and the Saudi aircrews are graduates of the best American and British flying schools.

A patrol of two F15-Cs from one of the RSAF's three interceptor squadrons; the pilots were trained to a high standard in the USA. *(Photo: Y.Debay)*

# AIR BRIDGE

The sheer scope of Operation 'Desert Shield', and the distance which separates the United States and Saudi Arabia, have required — and still require — the employment of a massive 'air bridge', perhaps greater than that constructed during the Vietnam War.

The Military Airlift Command has at its disposal 83 C-5 Galaxy, 250 C-141 Starlifter and 281 C-130 Hercules transport aircraft. Additionally, the Air National Guard and Air Force Reserve units can provide another 44 C-5s, 16 C-141s and 380 C-130s at need.

The transports of the MAC can fly the Atlantic route between eastern US bases and Saudi Arabian airfields in about 18 hours. The Pentagon has calculated that 1,092 Starlifter flights are required to airlift a complete division of 12,800 men; a brigade of 2,000 men needs 273 Starlifter missions.

Washington has also requisitioned many aircraft from American civil airlines. In less than four weeks between mid-August

(Above) Lockheed C-5A Galaxy. These immense aircraft can carry 355 troops or two M60 tanks. *(Photo: Y.Debay)*

(Below) The other heavy transport used by the MAC is the C-141 Starlifter, which can carry nearly 200 troops. *(Photo: E.Micheletti)*

and mid-September some 60,000 men were flown out to the Gulf in MAC and civilian aircraft; and by the end of September, just under two months after the start of American intervention, some 120,000 men had arrived in the Gulf by air. It is estimated that during the first weeks 'Desert Shield' demanded the commitment of more than 70% of the US armed forces' total air transport assets.

# THE SCREAMING EAGLES

Just unloaded from a fast transport ship, the warhorse of the 101st Airborne Division (Air Assault): the UH-60 Black Hawk helicopter. *(Photo: E. Micheletti)*

The CH-47 Chinook has been the faithful workhorse of the American armed forces since the early days of the Vietnam War in the mid-1960s; it has seen service in every US military intervention since then, and is flown by many overseas armies and air forces. With a basic payload of six tons or more than 30 fully equipped troops (figures grossly exceeded in combat emergencies before now), the CH-47 is strong, reliable, and very versatile. It can carry a wide range of internal and externally slung loads, including field artillery pieces for rapid battlefield redeployment. These CH-47s of the 101st have just been unloaded at Damman, and are still protected by travel covers. *(Photos: E.Micheletti)*

(Right) Black Hawks of the 101st lift off for the flight to the division's reception and transit base. This all-purpose battlefield helicopter can carry eleven fully equipped infantrymen at more than 190 mph, or can lift a slung load of 8,000 lbs. *(Photo: Y.Debay)*

(Below) On the quayside at Damman, Black Hawk crewmen rejoin their mount, already refitted for flight. Note the historic 'screaming eagle' patch of the 101st worn on their flight suits. *(Photo: Y.Debay)*

# US MARINES IN AN OCEAN OF SAND

**Somewhere in the Arabian sands, a US Marine unit mounted in LVTP-7 Amtracs complete a leg of their march, and NCOs gather round their officers for debriefing.**
*(Photo: Y.Debay)*

(Above) Command post of a Marine battalion of the 1st MEB, rigged around the LVTP-7s which carry the Leathernecks over sand as easily as over water.

(Left) One problem that does not arise in the desert is radio communications: the terrain offers no obstacles to clear transmission.

(Opposite) The M198 towed howitzer can fire four 155mm rounds a minute out to ranges of up to 30 kilometers with rocket-assisted ammunition.

(Photos: Y.Debay)

The US Marine Corps — whose equipment, organisation, peacetime deployment and training are all configured with exactly this type of crisis in mind — is naturally well represented in the Gulf. The main units on the ground are three large Marine Expeditionary Brigades, made up of units from as far afield as Hawaii and North Carolina, and totalling some 45,000 Leathernecks under the command of Maj. Gen. John Monahan.

An MEB is a task force composed of varying numbers and types of units according to the mission; its strength can vary between 8,000 and 18,000, but it includes between two and five regiments of Marine infantry, an artillery regiment, and battalion-sized supporting units. It has an air group of some 70 fixed-wing and 100 rotary-wing aircraft; can operate from ships, by airlift, or in any combination of the two; and is normally transported on some 20 ships, along with completely independent supplies for some 30 days.

Disembarked in mid-August at the port of Al-Jubayl, the Marines now have all their heavy equipment in place: 200 LVTP-7s, 100 M60A1 Patton tanks, six 155mm M109 and six 203mm M110A2 self-propelled artillery pieces, and some 50 towed pieces. They are supported by Marine air assets including F-18 Hornet fighters and AV-8B Harrier V/STOL fighter-bombers. Helicopters include CH-46E Sea Knights, CH-53E Super Stallions, and AH-1T Cobras. About half of these choppers are based on four heli-

copter carriers cruising a few miles off the Saudi coast: the USS *Inchon*/LPH-12 (carrying the 26th Marine Expeditionary Unit), the USS *Guam*/LPH-9, USS *Iwo Jima*/LPH-2, and USS *Nassau*/LHA-4.

These vessels are accompanied by about 14 other transport and escort ships. The 45,000 Marines of the three MEBs and their back-up are integrated into the 7th Marine Expeditionary Force. Another 10,600 Marines are also at sea on vessels cruising the coasts of Oman and Yemen to the south. Since late October the Marines ashore have enjoyed the armored support of the British 7th Armd. Bde., with two regiments of Challenger tanks, an armored infantry battallion, and further artillery assets.

Marine Expeditionary Brigade personnel disembark by helicopter. This is the CH-53E Super Stallion, the most powerful of Western helicopters; it can haul 16 tons of payload, which enables it to handle some 93% of the US Marines' fighting equipment. *(Photo: Y.Debay)*

# DESERT TRACKS

(Left) The LVTP-7 is called the 'Marine taxi'; totally amphibious without preparation, it carries 25 fully equipped Marines right from the loading dock of an assault ship to the beach, and up it into the developing beachhead. It has been greatly improved since the more vulnerable early marks served in Vietnam. Amtrac units are available to all Marine Expeditionary Units down to battalion size.

(Left below) The US Army is in the process of conversion to the M2 Bradley Infantry Fighting Vehicle, but still employs numbers of the veteran M113 armored personnel carrier. These GIs of the 197th Infantry Brigade prefer to ride the roof when outside the immediate combat zone.

(Below and right) Each US Marine Artillery Regiment has, in its 5th Battalion, twelve self-propelled M110A2 howitzers. These massive pieces can throw a 203mm shell out to 21 kilometers, or 29 km with rocket-assisted rounds. The Marine gunner's confidence is understandable. *(Photos: Y.Debay)*

# WITH THE ABRAMS OF TH

Damman quayside, in the last days of August 1990: *'Here they are!'* Gen. Norman Schwarzkopf was watching the first M1 Abrams tanks emerging from the USS *Denebola* — and with some relief. Without heavy armor the first elements of the US expeditionary force had been a shield more in name than in reality. Since Arnhem in 1944 it has been accepted: paratroopers cannot beat a determined tank attack — and Saddam Hussein is supposed to have 5,000 of them. The small reconnaissance force of elderly, lightweight Sheridans fielded by the 82nd Airborne could not have stood up against the Iraqi T-72s for long; and even with their excellent modern light anti-tank weapons the quick-reaction units of the 82nd and 101st would soon have been desperately hard pressed by a major armored offensive.

The arrival of the first M1s of the 64th Armored Regiment may not have made much difference to the odds in terms of simple number-counting; but they were the vanguard of a much more formidable force — and Saddam knew it.

Their tracks tearing up the tarmac of the quay, the Abrams ground away towards the main gate of the ultra-modern port built by King Abdul Aziz, where Saudi army tank-transporters stood waiting. The tank crews, flown in a week before by Galaxy, already sported on their new desert camouflage fatigues the round shoulder patch bearing the Hawaian taro-leaf, symbol of the 24th Infantry Division (Mechanised). The 24th 'Victory' Division is the principal heavy division of the US Third Army, attached to XVIII Airborne Corps, the higher formation of America's rapid deployment forces.

A week later we joined troops of the division in the deep desert. For obvious security reasons we cannot say exactly where Col. Kern, second in command of the 2nd Bde., had set up his command post

42

# VICTORY' DIVISION

of three M577 armored carriers. Each of these command versions of the M113 APC has its own function: in-coming intelligence, liaison with supporting arms, and co-ordination of out-going orders. Three hours' driving brought us to the command post, whose brigade was deployed some 50 miles from the Iraqi border, in the second line behind the Arab contingents of the multi-national force. In the shade of a camouflage net, Col. Kern explained his mission:

'Our primary mission is deterrent. We are here to signal to the guys over there that if they invade, they'll have a fight on their hands. Our secondary mission, obviously, is to protect the territorial integrity of Saudi Arabia, alongside the Royal Saudi Army and the Pan-Arab force. Ultimately, of course, we are soldiers and we obey orders: if we are so ordered, we will move on Kuwait City.'

The 2nd Bde. of the 24th Div., normally based at Fort Stewart, Georgia, comprises two battalions of mechanised infantry with M2 Bradleys, and two battalions of M1 Abrams tanks. Its base of fire is provided by a self-propelled artillery battalion with M109 howitzers; and Col. Kern can also call up the terrible firepower of 203mm M110 self-propelled howitzers, and M270 MLRS — multiple rocket launchers capable of pulverising targets at more than 18 miles' range, spreading hundreds of sub-munitions over a wide area. 'We'll really need them if it comes to a fight — they've got massive artillery assets over there', the colonel added.

A few moments later we clambered onto a Humvee and moved off towards the front line positions. The desert is almost featureless — we followed the traces left by previous wheels and tank tracks. From time to time the vehicle passed through an area where the air seemed even hotter than usual: it was like a burning slap in the face. We passed position after position, the combat vehicles deployed for all-round defense under the thin shelter of camouflage nets.

Under the brazen hammer of the sun, nothing moved; only the occasional camel could be seen, browsing on the sparse clumps of thorn. But the calm was deceptive; in a few seconds an M1 could throw off its camouflage and unleash its awesome firepower.

In a cloud of dust the Humvee drew up alongside two M577s, the command post of Maj. Barrett, commanding Task Force 3/15: a company of Bradleys from the 3rd Bn., 15th Infantry, and two companies of M1 tanks from the 1/64th Armor.

In the relative shade of a net a group of Rangers attached to the 24th had just returned from patrol. On an ammo box stood a few bottles of *Nissah* (a brand of Saudi water which has become one of the trademarks of 'Desert Shield') wrapped in damp scarves. 'The evaporation keeps the water cooler', grinned a Chicano trooper from Los Angeles — 'it only gets to about

A 'hedgehog' of M1 Abrams tanks and M2 Bradley IFVs of the 24th Infantry Division (Mechanised) stand guard in the Arabian desert, ready for anything the Iraqis choose to attempt. Tank for tank the Abrams is more than a match for even the late-model T-72s of the Iraqi armored divisions.
*(Photo: Y. Debay)*

The American armor is covered with camouflage netting whenever possible, but can be ready for combat in a matter of seconds. This is an Abrams of the 1/64th Armor, 24th Inf.Div. *(Photo: Y.Debay)*

80°!' 'It's just a little cooler than the tea we offered those Bedouin last night' added a big black Ranger from Mississippi.

The 24th is adapting itself little by little to life in the desert. The commanders have even ordered tracked vehicle drivers to try to avoid destroying the meagre clumps of camel-thorn: the Bedouin notice, and appreciate the gesture.

At about 4 p.m. the heat begins to relent slightly, and the desert slowly comes alive. A platoon of M1s get under way; the cornering tracks throw up fountains of sand, the turrets turn quickly, and the stabilised 105mm guns sway dangerously, like cobras ready to strike. During a pause the crewmen loll in the open hatches.

'Man, this heat . . . It was nothing like this even in the Mojave', grunts a Mid-Western tanker. The only troopers who were slightly acclimatised were the gunners of the 341st Artillery, who were caught by the Gulf crisis in the middle of training in the California desert. Their M109s were rapidly embarked for the Middle East, and the men were lifted almost directly from one desert to another in Boeing 747s.

The tankers are very proud of their mounts. They are confident that the M1 can handle the Iraqi T-72; and this confidence in the quality of US equipment is echoed wherever you go among the units of the task force. Morale is high; the GIs make no secret of wanting to get the job done, so they can be home for Christmas.

Despite the stereotype GI's love of extravagant comforts, which figures in so many half-envious European jokes, the American troops holding the desert front line are putting up with conditions as rugged as can be imagined — and will fight the better for it, if it comes to a fight. There is no air-conditioning out here, no showers, and no iced Coke. Only the rear-echelon troops who unload the Galaxies back at Dhahran can hope for such luxury. Here, an Abrams crew sleep on top of their tank, and live on three MREs — dehydrated 'Meals Ready to Eat', or combat ration packs — every day. Water stays fresh only for the hour after dawn.

The questions the men ask their officers are the same that soldiers ask the world over: 'What's going on? What are we going to do next?' In a generation used to mass-

ive media input the modern soldier is hungry for information. The GIs love to hear the latest news, and snatch up any paper or magazine which comes their way. In Maj. Barrett's words: 'For the first time in history, common soldiers know that they are playing a part in hugely important events. The great American press has a duty to support its soldiers, and not to repeat the mistakes of Vietnam. If it does, there's no reason why the American soldiers engaged in 'Desert Shield' shouldn't be victorious.'

An enormous blood-red sun sinks slowly towards the horizon, painting the sand-colored tanks glowing pink. A breath of hot wind rustles a clump of camel-thorn. The desert closes in on itself once again; but in the night the men of the 'Victory' Division still await their moment. They are ready.

# ABRAMS M1 MAIN BATTLE TANK

**Crew:** Four
**Total weight:** 53 tons
**Maximum speed:** 45 mph
**Range of action:** 280 miles
**Height:** 9.5 ft.
**Length:** 26 ft.
**Armament:** One 105mm M68A1 cannon

(55 rounds stowed); one .50 and two 7.62mm MGs
**Powerplant:** Lycoming AGT-1500 gas turbine (fuel consumption, approx 1.8 gals./mile on road, to 3.5 gals/mile cross-country)
**Protection:** 'Chobham' type composite armor, details classified.

The Abrams, together with the veteran M60A1 of the US Marine Expeditionary Brigades, forms the armored backbone of the American intervention force. The markings on the skirt armor are tactical insignia identifying the sub-units. *(Photo: E.Micheletti)*

Abrams of the 'Victory Division' at speed — 40 mph — in the Arabian desert, throwing up plumes of fine sand. *(Photo: Y.Debay)*

# THE PATRIOT

Patriot surface-to-air missile system photographed at Damman port. This system can counter every kind of aerial threat up to and including Iraq's 'Scud' surface-to-surface missiles. *(Photo: Y.Debay)*

One of the newest pieces of equipment shipped to the Gulf is the Patriot ground-to-air missile system, successor to the Nike, Hercules, and Hawk systems. It has been many years in development, but is judged to be well worth waiting for: its efficiency, even in high temperatures, is rated highly. It is deployed in quadruple sets of containers on a heavy launch vehicle; and can be fitted

**Length:** 16.9 ft.
**Diameter:** 1.3 ft.
**Powerplant:** Thiokol TX-486 solid fuel rocket
**Range:** approx. 50km
**Speed:** approx. Mach 3

with a conventional explosive or fragmentation or a nuclear warhead. Its most important component is its radar system, which performs all target acquisition, surveillance, pursuit and guidance functions. Its most important potential targets in the Gulf are Iraq's 'Scud' missiles: Iraqi propaganda makes bold claims for locally improved versions of this Soviet-supplied surface-to-surface system.

The Royal Saudi forces have several batteries of 127mm Astros II rocket-launchers made in Brasil. These surface-to-surface missiles are used for saturation fire on the battlefield.

*(Photo: Y.Debay)*

# ALLIED ARAB FORCES

At a dug-in command post in the front lines Saudi soldiers display the Heckler & Koch MP-5 sub-machine gun which is issued to all Saudi motorised infantry. This proven 9mm German weapon is popular for its compactness and reliability. *(Photos: Y.Debay)*

# THE ROYAL SAUDI ARMED FORCES

(Below and previous page) Men of the Saudi National Guard armed with G-3 rifles struggle through an assault course at a desert training camp. *(Photos: E.Micheletti)*

On the north-east frontier of the kingdom the Royal Saudi Army is deployed in considerable strength. Motorised and armored units have dug themselves into defensive lines in the deep desert. The armored 'hedge-hogs' are protected against air attack by powerful batteries of Crotale and Shahine missiles. The Saudi brigades have occupied positions some 40 miles from the furthest point of advance of the Iraqi forces inside Kuwait, so as to avoid risking any incident which might provoke irreparable consequences. The Royal Saudi Army has two armored brigades, one equipped with American vehicles including M60A1s and A3s, the other with French armor: AMX-30 tanks and AMX-109 armored personnel carriers.

The Saudis also deploy four mecha-

Saudi tank crews man French-supplied AMX-30S main battle tanks dug into hull-down hides near the desert frontier. Although the fatigues are American, the crew helmets are French F-1 models supplied with the tanks. *(Photos: E. Micheletti)*

nised brigades with equipment purchased from the USA, France, and Brazil. There is an infantry brigade stationed in the interior of the country; and an airmobile brigade, kept as a final reserve.

Apart from well-equipped troops, the kingdom has another major resource in case of Iraqi agression: the massive strategic depth represented by the huge open spaces of Saudi Arabia. At the least sign of enemy movement, which would be naked to the watchful AWACS and surveillance satellites, the Saudi, US, and allied air forces could be over the battlefield in 15 minutes.

A counterstroke would be supported by Saudi Arabia's modern artillery, notably the 224 self-propelled 155mm M109s, and 50 of the

formidable French GCT 155mm AuF-1 guns, capable of destroying whole units in moments.

The ultimate resource lies in the Saudi soldiers' knowledge of the deceptively empty terrain, and their inborn ability to live in the desert, and to use it. As a Saudi officer said: 'Everyone here knows how to put a pebble under his tongue, and keep going without water.'

# AMX-30

Classic study of an AMX-30S, the specially adapted hot-climate export version of this long-serving French tank. The Saudis have about 300 of them, serving in one armored and two motorised brigades. *(Photo: E.Micheletti)*

The Saudi tank units are trained in a technique used widely throughout the Middle East, where natural cover is scarce. Tanks are dug-in, in hides constructed by bulldozers, leaving only the camouflaged turret and gun above ground level. A single burst of engine power brings them up to the desert surface again, fully mobile, if manoeuver is required. *(Photos opposite: Y. Debay.)*

## AMX-30 MAIN BATTLE TANK
### (Tropicalised 'S' variant)

**Crew:** Four
**Total weight:** 35.5 tons
**Maximum speed:** 40 mph
**Range of action:** 400 miles

**Length:** 21.6 ft. **Height:** 9.2 ft.
**Armament:** One 105mm cannon, one
.50 and one 7.62mm MGs
**Powerplant:** Hispano-Suiza diesel, 700 hp.

# 'ASKARI! HOUW!'

On the great parade ground of King Fah'd Military City the cry of 'Askari! Houw!' ('Soldiers — Attention!') rings out dozens of times on this hot mid-September afternoon. The kingdom is in peril, and thousands of civilian volunteers have come forward to enlist in armed forces which are normally purely professional. For the first time in its history Saudi Arabia openly appealed to national sentiment; and the call was heeded. The numbers are classified, but since the beginning of the crisis some 500 men a day have come forward to join territorial units in defense of their country.

Naturally, the Royal Army is unable to turn these merchants, artisans, lawyers, and students into soldiers overnight. But every day the volunteers spend two hours training at one of the many camps and barracks all over the country; their families often come too, to watch a father or a son being drilled. When they have completed basic training the volunteers will guard industrial targets and carry out security patrols, freeing regular units for the front.

The volunteers pounding the square this afternoon at King Fah'd Military City are of all ages and many backgrounds. The oldest, a splendid white-bearded figure, is 71 years old and has 11 grandchildren. He says simply, 'I am an old man, so I have no fear of death.' The youngest is just 14; no, his parents did not try to talk him out of enlisting — he says they are proud of him.

The drill session continues, each movement punctuated by the staccato shouts of the instructors. One fat volunteer is visibly suffering, but grits his teeth. Two others, majestically bearded in the time-honored masculine fashion of their ancient warrior tribe, perform each movement with perfect precision. They have been under training for two weeks; tomorrow, they are proud to report, they will begin weapons training. Another platoon, composed of younger men, have already received their G-3 rifles.

The call of the *muezzin* interrupts the training session. The volunteers kneel and begin their devotions. Tomorrow, and every other day, they will come here again for two hours. The Holy Cities of Mecca and Medina, sacred above all other Islamic holy places, will not fall into the hands of the cynical atheist Saddam while these men protect them.

The Royal Saudi Army is an entirely regular, professional, volunteer force; it is well paid, and well trained by Western instructors. *(Photo: E.Micheletti)*

# THE EGYPTIAN CONTINGENT

J ust over a week after the Iraqi invasion of Kuwait, Egypt sent the first battalion of an initial 5,000-strong force to support Saudi Arabia. Among the first troops to be committed were an airmobile Commando brigade, 2,000 strong, flown to Saudi Arabia in Antonov transports and Boeing airliners. Lightly equipped, they are nevertheless troops of élite quality. A few days later an infantry brigade followed. Early in September Cairo announced that the force would be increased to a total of 20,000, and by the middle of the month the movement by sea and air was well under way: troops, light armor, M60 and T-62 tanks, and artillery. In all some 6,000 of the total are airborne and other special forces units.

The front line of defense on the Saudi borders is a Saudi-commanded force of about 40,000 including some 16,000 non-Saudi Arab troops. Here the Egyptian Commandos serve alongside men from the United Arab Emirates, Oman, Morocco, Syria, Qatar, Bahrain, and Kuwait.

**(Above) The Egyptian Commando brigade retain Soviet-supplied helmet, weapon and equipment but wear a new national camouflage uniform.** *(Photo: E.Micheletti)*

**(Below) Though only equipped with light weapons and vehicles in keeping with their role, the Egyptian Commandos have useful numbers of TOW and Milan launchers.** *(Photo: E.Micheletti)*

Two months of Spartan existence in the Saudi desert have not damaged the Commandos' morale; for them, acclimatisation to deep desert conditions is infinitely easier than for Western troops. Their equipment is simple, but well adapted to the terrain and their mission. *(Photo: Y.Debay)*

(Below) The standard weapon of the Commandos is still the ubiquitous AK-47, here in an Egyptian-made folding-stock version. *(Photo: Y.Debay)*

# OTHER ARAB, ISLAMIC, AND THIRD WORLD CONTINGENTS

Every day since the beginning of the Gulf Crisis has brought further promises of reinforcement for Saudi Arabia and other threatened Gulf states from non-Western governments. Totals are hard to calculate, but it seems that the eventual number of troops present from non-Western overseas armies may approach 80,000. The difficulty of reaching exact figures lies in the different reported destinations, arrival dates, and exact terms of service of these contingents.

Cautiously, then: it seems that **Morocco** has sent a mechanised brigade (1,200 men) to Saudi Arabia, with another 2,000 (perhaps 5,000) elsewhere or promised. **Pakistan** has sent or promised three infantry and one artillery battalions and logistic units totalling 5,000, and already has 1,000 advisers present. **Bangladesh** has promised 5,000, but with limitations on their use. Some 2,000 **Senegalese** are reportedly promised. A mechanised brigade of **United Arab Emirate** and **Omani** soldiers is in place (3,000 men), as are contingents from **Qatar** and **Bahrain**; the difficulty here is uncertainty over how many Gulf state troops will actually be sent to Saudi Arabia, as opposed to remaining in home defense posture but officially supporting the Saudi stance. From occupied **Kuwait** a few thousand men are now regrouped with Saudi front line forces. The most important single contribution may be from **Syria**, which has sent at least 14,000 men and 300 tanks, and may possibly commit many more.

A good view of the Commandos' shoulder patch and title, worn on the Egyptian camouflage fatigues by a major (note shoulder slide ranking) holding the unit flag. Older members of this unit fought in Sinai in 1973, where the helicopter-inserted Commandos earned Israel's ungrudging respect. The Commandos are organised into 1,000-man Groups, numbered from 127th upward, each divided into four sub-units.
(Photo: E.Micheletti)

(Above) Gasmask drill for men of a Syrian unit in Saudi Arabia; note Soviet-made equipment and AK-47s. Desert conditions would, in practice, prevent lengthy use of masks or NBC suits by men exerting themselves in any way: heat exhaustion would quickly fell them.

(Left) These Syrian special forces were apparently airlifted straight from Lebanon, where they have long experience of active service in that wretched country's interminable civil wars, to the Saudi Arabian front lines. *(Photos: Y.Debay)*

# THE SYRIAN COMMANDOS

Since September 1990 Damascus has been moving units into Saudi Arabia at the Kingdom's request to help confront Saddam Hussein — long President Assad's bitterest rival as leader of the Arab powers. The core of this force is the 9th Armored Division with some 14,000 men, 300 tanks, motorised infantry, artillery, and supporting arms. In addition, Soviet Air Force Antonovs have airlifted in several battalions of commandos.

These Special Forces — *al-Wahdat al-Khassa* — are grouped, with Syria's parachute units, into a single division of some 18,000 men divided between nine regiments. Though their organisation is Soviet, their tactical

role is more like that of their Egyptian counterparts: in the offensive they are employed as shock assault units to break gaps in the enemy line; in the defensive, as anti-tank units lavishly equipped with portable missile launchers, to seal off enemy armored thrusts.

More than half the Syrian army's effectives are regulars; the Special Forces have a particularly high reputation for determination and professionalism, and many units have been seasoned in combat in Lebanon. All these commandos are thought to be recruited from the Alawite sect of Islam, to ensure loyalty to the Alawite President Assad's regime.

# ON RECCE WITH THE 'ALL-AMERICANS'

(Opposite) In the blinding desert light, a column of Sheridans from the 82nd Airborne's light tank battalion — the 3/73rd Armor — redeploy.

(Background) A scene recalling the Libyan campaigns of Rommel and Montgomery: at the point where a tiny oasis provides almost the only feature higher than thorn-scrub to break the horizon, a reconnaissance unit sets up its command post. *(Photos: E.Micheletti)*

(Above) The 82nd Airborne is America's only fully para-qualified formation: the 'All-American' patch and title are proudly displayed.

# HUMVEE: ANY JOB, ANYWHERE

In 1983 the AM General Division of LTV Aerospace and Defense offered the Pentagon a vehicle intended to replace the Ford M151 Mutt, M274 Mule and M792 Ambulance, and the 2½-ton light truck. The new vehicle was designated HMMWV ('High Mobility Multi Weapons Vehicle'), which the manufacturers clipped to 'Hummer', and the GIs soon christened 'Humvee'. From the end of 1985 large numbers were acquired and issued to all types of American units — there are already some 80,000 in service.

The Humvee exists in a number of different versions: troop transport, command vehicle, signals, fire support, ambulance, reconnaissance, and anti-tank — with TOW missile launchers. A recent development now coming into service is the 'Red-T' — 'Remote Electric Drive Turret' — more often called the Bushmaster Carrier. This has a turret or barbette mounting the Hughes Bushmaster 25mm 'chain gun', with a rate of fire of 2,000 rpm, as mounted on the M2 and M3 Bradley Infantry and Cavalry Fighting Vehicles.

**(Left) On the tarmac of Dhahran airbase a USAF Humvee mounts (shrouded here) the redoubtable Mk. 19 40mm automatic grenade launcher.** *(Photos: E.Micheletti)*

## HIGH MOBILITY MULTI WEAPONS VEHICLE

**Maximum weight:** 8,530 lbs.
**Maximum speed:** 65.25 mph
**Range:** 310 miles
**Height:** 7.4 ft. **Length:** 14.9 ft.
**Width:** 7 ft. **Clearance:** 1.3 ft.
**Powerplant:** General Motors/ Chevrolet THM 400 HD

(Opposite top) Head-on view of the Humvee, the US forces' new 'maid of all work'. Wing codes identify 24th Division, 3rd Bn. of 15th Inf. Regt.; and vehicle 5 of the HQ company.

(This page, and opposite center) Fire support Humvee of the 82nd Airborne, its temperate zone camouflage paint streaked with pale mud in testimony to the speed with which the division deployed to the desert.

61

# M551 SHERIDAN: FROM THE PADDY-FIELDS OF VIETNAM TO THE SANDS OF ARABIA

Even under the palm-trees the heat is always oppressive; but by now Capt. Bob Johnson, commanding Alpha Company of 3/73rd Armor, is used to it. Since mid-August his battalion — the armored reconnaissance element of 82nd Airborne — have carried out an intensive series of exercises and recce missions to accustom the 'para-tankers' to the terrain in which they may have to fight. They are now desert experts: by good luck, the order which sent them on to the Galaxies for the Middle East caught them during a desert training exercise in the Mojave.

The Sheridan is 'old — but damned good!', according to the airborne tankers. Although its aluminium armor (which is the secret of its light weight, and air-portable capability) is vulnerable to modern weapons, it has a fine turn of speed to get itself out of trouble. And the Iraqi T-72s would do well to stay out of range of its massive 152mm cannon, which gives tremendous killing-power (and has a recoil to match).

Many of the problems which dogged early marks of the Sheridan in the Vietnam War — electrical failures, cooling and filter failures, and complications due to the revolutionary 'self-consuming' propellant charge of the caseless ammunition — have long since been solved. Judged as an agile, hard-hitting scout tank rather than a main battle type, it has many strengths.

The recce unit of the 82nd Airborne fields 43 Sheridan light tanks. The M551 has been greatly improved since the Vietnam War, where a combination of over-hasty deployment of a revolutionary design, and wet tropical conditions, led to a host of reliability problems. The Sheridan is fast and agile; has a very powerful gun; and can be 'LAPESed' — air-dropped by parachute extraction from a very low-flying C-130 Hercules, with shock-absorbing packing to break its fall. *(Photo: E. Micheletti)*

(Right) The Sheridan has a four-man crew: commander, driver, gunner and loader. In these conditions all except the driver prefer to ride outside. *(Photo: E. Micheletti)*

## M551 SHERIDAN LIGHT RECONNAISSANCE TANK

**Crew:** Four
**Total weight:** 15 tons
**Maximum speed:** 43 mph
**Range of action:** 375 miles
**Height:** 7.5 ft. **Length:** 20.6 ft.
**Armament:** One 152mm cannon, one .50 and one 7.62mm MGs
**Powerplant:** Detroit 6V 53T diesel, 300 hp.

# THE 'LAV': OVER THE DUNES AT 60 MPH

The new 'thoroughbred mount' of the US Marine Corps has been giving the paratroopers of the 82nd Airborne ideas. Like their comrades in arms of the Marine Expeditionary Units, the 'All-Americans' need an air-transportable light armored vehicle, fast enough to punch through the enemy lines and spread havoc on his flanks and in the rear areas. The 'Light Attack Vehicle', a 10-ton eight-wheeler with a maximum road speed of about 70 mph, fits the bill.

Apart from its armament — a 25mm 'chain gun' cannon, and two 7.62mm machine guns — it has another advantage. Each vehicle can carry four to six fully equipped infantrymen in its armored hull — an obvious 'plus' for recce units otherwise equipped with Sheridan tanks.

For these reasons the 82nd Airborne have added a scout platoon mounted in the LAV to the divisional reconnaissance element. The mission to Saudi Arabia will provide the perfect testing ground for the new sub-unit, vehicle and tactics.

(Above and left) Men of the 82nd Airborne's scout platoon on a desert mission in their new LAV armored vehicles. The troopers can quickly disembark — note large rear doors — to deal with any troublesome pocket of resistance, covered by the LAV's 25mm 'chain gun' cannon. Again, note 'expedient camouflage' of smeared mud on these rapidly-shipped vehicles. *(Photo: Y. Debay)*

(Right) Dawn patrol along the vital desert highway which leads — eventually — to Kuwait City. One day soon, perhaps the LAVs will be opening this road for real . . . *(Photo: E. Micheletti)*

Printed in the United States of America

This edition published in Great Britain 1991 by
Windrow & Greene Ltd.,
5 Gerrard St., London W1V 7LJ

**British Library Cataloguing in Publication Data**
Micheletti, Eric
   Operation Desert Shield: the first 90 days. –
   (Europa-militaria)
   1. Persian Gulf countries. Military operations
   I. Title   II. Debay, Yves   III. Series
   953.6

**ISBN 1-872004-01-6**

**Acknowledgements:**
The authors wish to record their sincere thanks to the
public relations services of the United States Army,
Navy, Air Force and Marine Corps; and to all the
officers and men who made their job easier in the Gulf.
In particular they would also wish to record their great
gratitude to the Embassy of the Kingdom of Saudi
Arabia in Paris; and to the staff of the Royal Saudi
Ministry of Information for expediting the essential
authorisations. The publishers wish to thank Pierre
Besnard of 'Le Poilu' for assistance with the illustration
on p.10.